FULL THROTTLE

KARTS

BY THOMAS K. ADAMSON

EPIC

BELLWETHER MEDIA • MINNEAPOLIS, MN

EPIC

EPIC BOOKS are no ordinary books. They burst with intense action, high-speed heroics, and shadows of the unknown. Are you ready for an Epic adventure?

This edition first published in 2019 by Bellwether Media, Inc.

For information regarding permission, write to Bellwether Media, Inc., Attention: Permissions Department, 6012 Blue Circle Drive, Minnetonka, MN 55343.

Library of Congress Cataloging-in-Publication Data

Names: Adamson, Thomas K., 1970- author.
Title: Karts / by Thomas K. Adamson.
Description: Minneapolis, MN : Bellwether Media, Inc., 2019. | Series: Epic. Full Throttle | Includes bibliographical references and index. | Audience: Ages 7-12.
Identifiers: LCCN 2018031913 (print) | LCCN 2018033449 (ebook) | ISBN 9781681036571 (ebook) | ISBN 9781626179332 (hardcover : alk. paper)
Subjects: LCSH: Karts (Automobiles)–Juvenile literature.
Classification: LCC TL236.5 (ebook) | LCC TL236.5 .A33 2019 (print) | DDC 629.228/5–dc23
LC record available at https://lccn.loc.gov/2018031913

Editor: Christina Leaf Designer: Jeffrey Kollock

Printed in the United States of America, North Mankato, MN

TABLE OF CONTENTS

LAST LAP PASS

SHORT RACES

Most kart races last between 10 and 45 minutes.

Engines buzz as small, fast karts zip around the track. Only two laps are left. One driver tries to pass the leader. But the leader will not let her through.

The driver in second place catches the leader on a turn. Their wheels rub together!

She hits the gas and speeds away. She raises a fist as she crosses the finish line. Off to the **victory lane**!

WHAT ARE KARTS?

Karts are small race cars. They race low to the ground. The fastest karts can reach 150 miles (241 kilometers) per hour. Drivers need quick **reflexes**!

Some kart races are on oval tracks. **Sprint tracks** and road courses twist and turn.

Nearly anyone can race karts. Some kart drivers are as young as age 5!

CAREER PATH

Karting can lead to a motorsports career. NASCAR champion Jeff Gordon got his start in kart racing.

People can try karts at **amusement parks**. These karts have protective bumpers.

THE HISTORY OF KARTS

Art Ingels and Lou Borelli built the first racing kart in 1956. They brought it to a popular racetrack in Pomona, California. People loved the small, quick racer. Karts soon became popular across southern California.

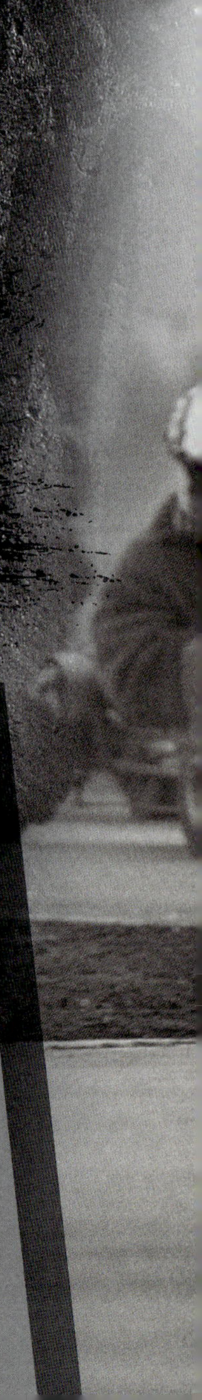

British Kart Championship, 1961

TRACK SURFACE

Kart races take place on dirt or paved tracks.

Rockford Kart Nationals, 1960

KART TIMELINE

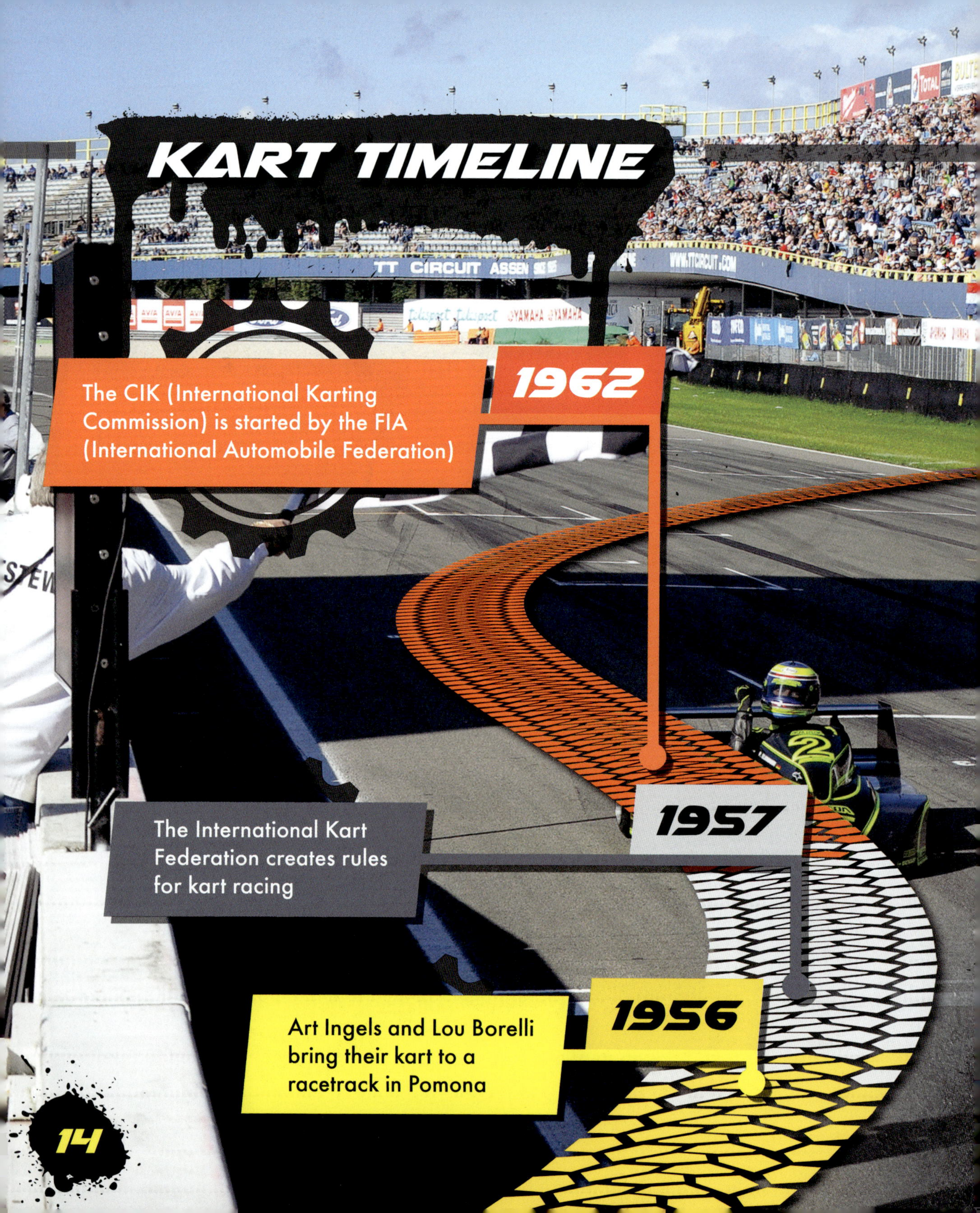

1962

The CIK (International Karting Commission) is started by the FIA (International Automobile Federation)

1957

The International Kart Federation creates rules for kart racing

1956

Art Ingels and Lou Borelli bring their kart to a racetrack in Pomona

Danica Patrick begins racing karts at age 10

1992

1980s

Jeff Gordon wins four karting championships

By the late 1950s, companies were building engines just for kart racing. The sport quickly spread around the world. There are now racing **leagues** in the United States, Europe, and Asia.

KART PARTS

Kart engines usually sit next to the driver. Engines are either gas or electric. Kart tires are small and wide. On dry, paved tracks, tires have no **tread**. Racers use **grooved** tires on wet tracks or dirt tracks.

SPEEDWAY KARTS

On speedway karts, the wheels are covered by the body. The driver sits lower for added speed.

21

Drivers must wear safety gear. Racing suits protect drivers from scrapes. Drivers also wear chest protectors. Neck supports protect the collarbone in crashes.

IDENTIFY A KART

KART COMPETITIONS

Kart racers compete in different **classes** based on age and skill. Drivers earn points in each race. The driver with the most points in a season wins the championship!

Karts are more than amusement park rides. They are serious racers!

GLOSSARY

amusement parks—places where people pay to go on rides, play games, and enjoy other forms of entertainment

classes—groups of racers divided up by age or skill level

grooved—having thin channels or lines

leagues—groups of people with a common interest

reflexes—actions or movements that happen without a person's control or effort

sprint tracks—paved tracks that have right and left turns; sprint tracks are generally 0.25 to 0.5 miles (0.4 to 0.8 kilometers) long.

tread—the ridges on a car tire that help it keep from slipping on a dirt road or a wet track

victory lane—the place at the racetrack where the winning driver is awarded the trophy and celebrates the win

TO LEARN MORE

AT THE LIBRARY

Challen, Paul. *Kart Racing.* New York, N.Y.: PowerKids Press, 2015.

Maddox, Jake. *Kart Competition.* North Mankato, Minn.: Stone Arch Books, 2014.

Mason, Paul. *Kart Racer: Lando Norris vs Callum Ilott.* New York, N.Y.: Franklin Watts, 2016.

ON THE WEB

FACTSURFER

Factsurfer.com gives you a safe, fun way to find more information.

1. Go to www.factsurfer.com.

2. Enter "karts" into the search box.

3. Click the "Surf" button and select your book cover to see a list of related web sites.

INDEX

The images in this book are reproduced through the courtesy of: PhotoMDP, front cover; PhotoStock10, pp. 4-5, 6, 7; Commission Internationale de Karting CIK/KSP/ cikfia media center, pp. 8-9, 9, 10, 14-15, 16-17, 20, 20-21; mariakraynova, p. 11; PA Images Archive/ Getty Images, p. 12; The Enthusiast Network/ Getty Images, pp. 12-13; Action Sports Photography, p. 15 (1992, 1980s); John Quixley - Australia/ Alamy, p. 16; avid_creative, pp. 18-19; Jibjeep_Photo, p. 19.